THE ST. LAWRENCE

THE ST. LAWRENCE

BY TRUDY J. HANMER

FRANKLIN WATTS
New York | London | Toronto | Sydney
1984 | A FIRST BOOK

Cover photograph courtesy of the
St. Lawrence Seaway Development Corporation

Map by Vantage Art, Inc.

Photographs courtesy of:
St. Lawrence Seaway Development Corporation: pp. 2, 34, 37;
The St. Lawrence Seaway Commission: p. 10;
Annan Photo Features: p. 12; The Bettmann Archive: pp. 16, 19, 24;
The Public Archives of Canada; p. 30; Michigan Travel Bureau: p. 31;
Ewing Galloway: pp. 40, 45, 46, 51; National Film Board: p. 56.

Library of Congress Cataloging in Publication Data
Hanmer, Trudy J.
The St. Lawrence.

(A First book)
Includes index.
Summary: Describes the Saint Lawrence River and its
effect on the geography, history, economy, and people of
the region through which it flows. Also discusses the
special problems of this waterway and its future prospects.
1. Saint Lawrence River—Juvenile literature.
2. Saint Lawrence River Valley—Juvenile literature.
[1. Saint Lawrence River.   2. Saint Lawrence River Valley.
3. Rivers] I. Title. II. Title: Saint Lawrence.
F1050.H36 1984   971.4   84-7251
ISBN 0-531-04831-4

CONTENTS

CHAPTER ONE
A Life on the River
1

CHAPTER TWO
The Land and the River
5

CHAPTER THREE
Early Inhabitants
14

CHAPTER FOUR
Political Development
21

CHAPTER FIVE
The Seaway
28

CHAPTER SIX
Economic Development
39

CHAPTER SEVEN
Ecology and the Seaway
48

CHAPTER EIGHT
The Future of the Waterway
54

Index
59

FOR PETER
AND CASEY

THE ST. LAWRENCE

CHAPTER ONE

A LIFE ON THE RIVER

Once a week from early April to mid-December, Claude Bigtree Michaud leaves his riverfront home in St.-Jean-Port-Joli. He travels by car to Pointe-au-Père where he boards an ocean freighter bound for the Great Lakes. Claude is a St. Lawrence river pilot, a man whose special job is to guide ocean-going ships safely up the St. Lawrence River, through the St. Lawrence Seaway, until their own captains take the wheel once again at the bottom of Lake Ontario.

Pilots like Claude are chosen because they know this river. They know its twists and turns and dangerous currents. These pilots are able to steer a ship through channels so narrow that sailors standing by the rail of the ship can talk to golfers putting on greens at one of the many golf courses along the banks of the beautiful river. Seaway pilots know exactly how to park the huge ships in locks where there are sometimes fewer than six inches to spare on each side of a ship as wide as a football field.

Claude, like most of the pilots, grew up on the shore of the St. Lawrence River. He has been learning the secrets of the river

all his life. His grandfather and his father were both river pilots, and he learned his earliest lessons about the river from them. His great-grandfather was a farmer and pilot who lived in Bic, Quebec. In the late 1800s these farmers raced each other to the shore to compete for jobs piloting the ships that passed by their farms. Unlike his great-grandfather, Claude knows ahead of time which ships he will pilot. He boards his freighters from a tugboat owned by the Canadian government.

Claude's family, like most families living along the Canadian side of the St. Lawrence River, is descended from the French people who began to come to the New World in the 1500s. Claude's first and last names are of French origin, but his middle name is a Mohawk name. Some of his ancestors were members of this tribe, a branch of the great Iroquois nation that inhabited the banks of the St. Lawrence long before the European explorers and settlers arrived. The Iroquois were the first people to understand and navigate the St. Lawrence River. Claude is proud of his Native American forebears. He feels that he is a better pilot because of the combination of river peoples in his background. In addition to his French and Mohawk ancestors, he is also related to a British seaman who entered the New World as part of the army of General James Wolfe, the man who conquered New France.

Claude is fifty years old. When he first began piloting ships on the St. Lawrence, river pilots navigated the channel according to landmarks. In the years since Claude became a pilot, the river has changed because of the development of the St. Lawrence Seaway. The ships that sail on it have changed, too. Now pilots use

*Skilled St. Lawrence River pilots
navigate ocean freighters
through the Seaway's tricky
channels and numerous locks.*

sophisticated technology to check shore markers at each turn. In spite of the new machines in use, Claude and many other river pilots still watch the shore for familiar landmarks—the shrine at Ste.-Anne-de-Beaupré; the chapel of the Ursuline Convent where the great Canadian hero Montcalm is buried; the pulp boats along the shore at Trois-Rivières; and the towering center of Montreal, a city built atop an extinct volcano.

Claude's part of the journey ends when the ship reaches Kingston, Ontario. Here on the site of a fort constructed by Count Frontenac in 1673, the St. Lawrence River meets Lake Ontario. The Royal Military College, where Claude's son is a cadet seaman, stands on the site of the original fort.

From Pointe-au-Père to Kingston, Claude has traveled some 200 miles (320 km). As long a distance as this seems, Claude has covered about a tenth of the great waterway that comprises the river and the five Great Lakes. From Kingston, ships sail smoothly on through Lake Ontario to Lake Erie into the three other large lakes deep in the midwestern heart of North America. It is no wonder that the Iroquois told Jacques Cartier, one of the river's earliest European explorers, that he had arrived at "the river that has no end."

CHAPTER TWO

THE LAND AND THE RIVER

The river that the Iroquois described to Jacques Cartier has an end—and it has a beginning. It is not surprising, however, that the river seemed endless to people living in the sixteenth century. Those who saw it for the first time, as well as those who had lived on its banks for generations before the arrival of the Europeans, could not imagine where it ended.

The St. Lawrence River is the fifteenth largest river in the world and the third largest in North America. In Canada only the Mackenzie River is longer, and in the United States only the Mississippi outdistances it. When the St. Lawrence River is considered along with the five Great lakes—Ontario, Erie, Huron, Michigan, and Superior—it becomes one of the world's greatest inland waterways. Together these lakes and this river span half the width of North America and drain an area of land equal in size to all of France and Great Britain.

The St. Lawrence has its *source* (the name given to a river's beginning) in the St. Louis River, which flows into the western end of Lake Superior. Its *mouth* (the name given to a river's end) is located over 2,300 miles (3,680 km) away in the Atlantic Ocean. The current from the small St. Louis River pulses through all of the Great Lakes, gathering force as it races over falls and rapids on its way to the ocean. Along the way the current is fed by other rivers, known as tributaries. Some of the biggest of these tributaries are the Ottawa, the Richelieu, and the Saguenay.

Water from an area of over 680,000 square miles (1,761,200 km) surrounding the river and the Great Lakes in both the United States and Canada is released to the sea through the St. Lawrence River. The surrounding land from which a river draws its water is known as the *drainage area*. The water from the drainage area runs off into the lakes and then is rushed by the river to the ocean. The river keeps the lakes from flooding the land. Almost two million gallons of water pour into the river every second from Lake Ontario, the easternmost of the Great Lakes.

Just as the river helps the lakes, the lakes also help the river. While the water is in the lakes, these bodies of water act as settling basins, sieves which help to keep the river free from silt. This makes the St. Lawrence a clear, clean river. Another benefit of the interaction between the Great Lakes and the river is the constant flow of the St. Lawrence. This means that the St. Lawrence rarely rises more than ten feet in any year. This is not true for other great rivers, such as the Nile River in Egypt, the Yangtze River in China, or the Mississippi River. To keep the flow of the St. Lawrence so steady, the river must push 246,000 cubic feet (6,888 cu m) of water into the sea every second. One person has calculated that this amounts to enough water to give every man, woman, and child in America over fifty baths every day.

When pilots, ship captains, and geographers talk about any river, they use the terms *below* and *above* to locate spots along the river. These terms can be confusing if you are looking at a map of the St. Lawrence. The river flows from the southwest to the northeast, and on a flat map it seems as though the northeastern, or ocean, end is "above" the southwestern, or lake, end. However, this is not true. The part of any river closest to its

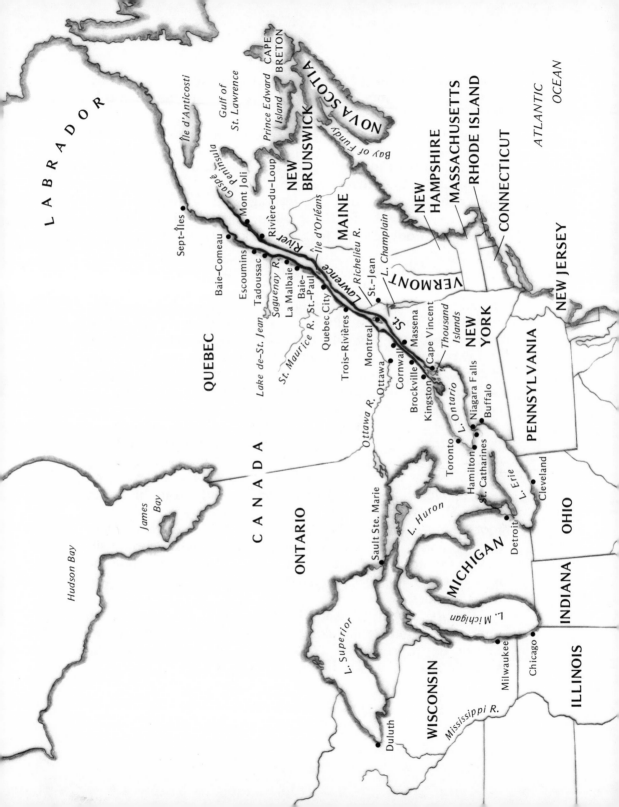

mouth is considered to be "below" the part of the river closest to its source. It is important to remember these terms when talking or reading about a river.

The St. Lawrence River is relatively young. It was formed during the last ice age. As the ice fields covering the North American continent began to move toward the Arctic Circle, they left behind glacier lakes that became the five Great Lakes. Geologists believe that about six thousand years ago, near the end of this ice age, a fault opened. The Great Lakes spilled out into the fault, creating the body of water that we now know as the St. Lawrence River.

If you were to taste the water in the river above Quebec City, it would not taste salty because from Montreal to Lake Ontario the St. Lawrence is a freshwater river. However, if you were to taste the river at St.-Jean-Port-Joli, where many of the river pilots live, it would taste salty, like the ocean. It is characteristic of the St. Lawrence River that it is a saltwater river for over 600 miles (960 km), from its mouth in the Gulf of St. Lawrence to an island, Île d'Orléans. This island lies in the middle of the river, just below Quebec City.

At Île d'Orléans fresh and salt water meet. People who live in the little towns along the edge of the island, St.-Pierre, St.-Laurent, St.-François, and Ste.-Famille, have grown used to having fresh water at low tide and salt water at high tide. Like large oceans, rivers that have salt water also have tides, and this is true of the St. Lawrence. Around Île d'Orléans there is a nineteen-foot (5.7-m) tide. At Quebec City the tide is reduced to 12½ feet (3.75 m), and at Trois-Rivières, a town above Quebec about halfway to Montreal, the tide is only 1 foot (.3 m). By the time the river reaches Montreal, it behaves like a normal freshwater river. It has no tides.

The presence of salt water in part of the St. Lawrence has an interesting effect on life along the river. Cows drinking at low tide on the shores of Île d'Orléans may see porpoises off the shore of that same island when the tide is high. St. Lawrence sportfishing is known worldwide. Freshwater bass and muskellunge are captured in the waters above Montreal. From this same river, world-renowned saltwater cod are taken from the water off the Gaspé Peninsula, near the river's mouth.

Ship captains have to be wary of the dual nature of the part-salt-, part-fresh-water river because a boat in salt water draws a foot less than a boat in fresh water. This means that a heavily loaded boat might navigate the river channel to Île d'Orléans safely, only to run aground in the fresh water above that island.

The salt water also affects whether or not the river freezes in winter. The climate is harsh all along the banks of the St. Lawrence, and winter temperatures in most places fall frequently below -30°F (-34°C). Below Quebec, however, the river hardly ever freezes; above Montreal it is frozen several months a year. Between Montreal and Quebec huge ships called icebreakers have kept the channel open almost all winter for most of the twentieth century. The spring thaw is a time for celebration. The first captain to get his ship through the ice from Quebec to Montreal each year receives a gold-headed cane as his reward.

This ceremony symbolizes the importance of the weather to the people living along the river. The broad part of the river from Quebec to the Gulf of St. Lawrence does not freeze. This is the river's *estuary*. (An estuary is the area of a river where the tide meets the river's current.) Unfortunately, this part of the river is the part that is least inhabited. Near the more populated areas along the river, the ice is sometimes as much as eighty feet (24 m) thick. It is in this area above Quebec, from Montreal to Canada's prairie provinces and the midwestern United States, that most of the people who depend on the river have always lived. Over one-fifth of Canada's population lives in the flatland along the freshwater portion of the river. Eight states of the United States touch this part of the river or the neighboring Great Lakes. These states account for nearly half of the nation's trading wealth.

An ocean-going vessel in one of Canada's
Beauharnois Locks. Icebreakers and ice-navigating
techniques keep shipping lanes open on the
St. Lawrence eight and a half months of the year.

Because of the richness of the flatland in the river valley, this part of the river has long attracted settlers. This area has also been, however, the most treacherous and least easily navigable stretch of the river. Going upstream from Quebec, ships run into Lake St. Peter, the first of three wide spots in the river so large that they are considered to be separate lakes. Above Lake St. Peter the river narrows again on its path toward Montreal. Around Montreal, early sailors, both Native American and European, met the first of the river's many *rapids.* (Rapids are areas of a river where the current moves very swiftly, breaking over large boulders and other obstacles in the riverbed.) In addition Montreal's harbor was long blocked by a strong current, St. Mary's Current, that prevented ships from entering the port without help. In earliest times ships were towed in by oxen. Later they were pushed and pulled by tugboats.

Above Montreal the river widens rapidly into two more lake areas, Lake St.-Louis and Lake St.-Francis. At the southern end of Lake St.-Francis the river enters the area known as the International Rapids. Here, until the Seaway was opened in 1959, boats were almost completely stopped. At the other end of the International Rapids, however, lies one of the most beautiful areas of the river. This is the Thousand Islands region, known by Native Americans as the "place where the Great Spirit dwells." This is the last section of the St. Lawrence River before its entry to the Great Lakes through Lake Ontario. No one agrees exactly how many islands dot the river here, but everyone agrees that there are more than one thousand. Some people believe that there may be as many as two thousand. There are small islands like Needle's Eye and Fiddler's Elbow and 10-mile- (16-km-) long islands like Wellesley Island. An unfinished, abandoned castle sits on one island. Other islands are home only to the blue heron and the red-winged blackbirds. Whatever their size, the islands dominate this 68-mile (109-km-) stretch of the river from Brockville to Kingston, Ontario, on the Canadian side and from Alexandria Bay to Cape Vincent, New York, on the American side.

It is here in the Thousand Islands that the river forms the border between the United States and Canada. This boundary has been an important factor in the history of these two nations, just as it was an important factor in the history of the European nations that gave birth to these two giant nations on the new continent.

The Thousand Islands region
in Alexandria Bay is one
of the most picturesque
spots on the St. Lawrence.

CHAPTER THREE

EARLY INHABITANTS

The first people to live along the banks of the St. Lawrence River had little use for boundaries. They were members of Native American tribes, especially those of the Iroquois and Algonquin nations. These people fished and hunted. They depended on the river for transportation and food. Although tribal warfare often disrupted their lives, ownership of the river was never the source of their quarrels. According to their folklore, the river "had no end." They believed that it was long enough to belong to all people. Anthropologists think that these tribal peoples had migrated from Siberia many thousands of years before any Europeans set foot in the "New World" of North America.

In 1534 Francis I, king of France, sent a sailor from the French village of Milo to search for a new passage to China. The French and other Europeans of this time greatly wanted to open up trade with the Orient. They had recently begun to believe that the world was round, not flat. With this thinking, it made sense to go West to look for a new water route to China. Jacques Cartier and his ships sailed into the Gulf of St. Lawrence in 1534.

Although Cartier did not go very far inland during this first trip, he claimed all of Canada for the French king. He met with Iroquois Chief Donnacona and persuaded or forced the chief to allow two of the chief's sons to return to France with Cartier.

On August 10, 1535, Cartier entered the Gulf of St. Lawrence for the second time. Because this date marked the feast of St. Lawrence, Cartier named the gulf for the saint. Originally Cartier named the river "River of Canada," but as time passed, other voyagers called the entire waterway by the one name of St. Lawrence.

By the end of his second voyage, Cartier had penetrated into the North American continent as far as Montreal (a village the Native Americans called Hochelaga). For a long time Cartier still believed he was on his way to China. The Lachine Rapids around Montreal, named by Cartier, are one indication of how strongly he believed he had found the Orient. *La Chine* means "China" in French. By the time he left to return to France, however, Cartier wrote in his diary that he believed he had found not the passage to the Indies, but "a midwest passage to the interiors of a vast continent."

Cartier returned to Canada once again in 1541. This time he was searching for gold and diamonds. Instead he found copper and quartz. In the last years of the 1500s, a few hearty French people traveled to North America, but they did not settle there. An early settlement on Cap Rouge failed after only a few months when the pioneers gave up and returned to France. During this time a legendary woman, Marguerite Roberval, survived for two and a half years after being abandoned by her uncle on an island in the St. Lawrence. She managed to flag a passing ship, which took her back to France, where she entertained her neighbors with tales of her adventures.

By 1600 the only significant settlement in "New France," as Canada had come to be called, was the trading post at Tadoussac. The true beginnings of European settlement came three years later with the arrival in the New World of Samuel de Champlain,

*In 1535 French explorer Jacques Cartier
encountered the Indians of Hochelaga, at
the site of present-day Montreal.*

another Frenchman. Unlike Cartier, Champlain was looking for Canada, not China. He made two preliminary voyages, in 1603 and 1605, before arriving in 1608 with a group of settlers. He called the area where he planned to settle, Quebec, from the Algonquin word *kebec,* meaning "narrows." Champlain's group was optimistic. They came expecting to stay and even planted rosebushes they had brought with them from France. Unhappily, by spring of the first year, only eight of the settlers were still alive, including their leader, Champlain.

Although his initial effort at settlement had failed in most respects, Champlain did not give up. By 1619 he had been appointed governor of the colony of Quebec, a position he held throughout much of the rest of his life. He died in 1635, one hundred years after Cartier first named the river that they had both sought to conquer.

By the time Champlain died, Roman Catholic priests from France, especially a sect called Jesuits, had arrived in Canada and were helping to settle the country. New French explorers were traveling even farther inland than Champlain had. After all, he had only gone as far as Lake Huron. A young man who had first come to Canada with Champlain, Étienne Brulé, was the first European to record having seen all five Great Lakes. Meanwhile, two other great French explorers, Marquette and Joliet, dreamed of finding a continuous connection between the St. Lawrence River and the Great Lakes. They wanted to bypass the falls and rapids. Yet another Frenchman, LaSalle, proved that people could go by water from the St. Lawrence River to the Gulf of Mexico. He was one of the *voyageurs,* French canoeists who paddled deep into the American wilderness, leaving all known settlement behind for years at a time.

Men like the voyageurs depended heavily on the knowledge and friendship of the Native American tribes. Yet it was the Roman Catholic missionaries who had the closest contact with the Iroquois, Huron, and Algonquins. As early as 1639 Madame de la Peltrie, known to the early settlers as Mère (or Mother)

Marie, tried to found a convent for Native American girls who wished to convert to Roman Catholicism.

Valuable as the Europeans found the help of the tribespeople, they still believed that European beliefs and ways of life were superior. As settlement progressed, the French tried to convert all the Native Americans to their religion, and they forced them to live under French law. British settlers would later make the same mistakes. By the 1640s, tension between the Native Americans and the European settlers had led to skirmishes between the two groups, especially the Mohawks and the French.

During this same time period a new breed of French fur trader emerged in the New World—the *coureur de bois.* Coureurs de bois traveled by canoe deep into the woods around the Great Lakes in search of beaver. At this time tall beaver hats for men had become fashionable in Paris, London, and other cities in Europe. Supplying the beaver pelts for these hats became the most income-producing business in Canada. Unfortunately the North American woods were almost depleted of beaver in the fur traders' attempts to make their fortunes by meeting the needs of this fashion.

The coureurs de bois were not settlers. They lived for months at a time alone on the water and came into trading-post villages like Trois-Rivières and Tadoussac only to sell the pelts they had collected. For this reason the fur trade did not add greatly to the numbers of settlers. Fishing and farming were the occupations that attracted Europeans who wanted to settle and make Canada their home. By 1665 there were over three thousand Europeans living in Canada.

A new chapter in the history of the settlement along the river began in the 1660s. British settlers arrived wishing to claim Canada for their king. For over half a century the British had been settling in villages along the Atlantic coast of what is now the United States. By the 1660s these people began to look north to the fertile fishing and farming in the St. Lawrence River valley. Back home in Europe the English and the French were not

French fur trappers, called coureurs de bois, *were on
friendly terms with the Native American population
as this etching by Frederick Remington suggests.
Unlike other European newcomers, the* coureurs de bois
*were after furs, not land, and so did not threaten
the Indians' territory or way of life.*

friends, and they carried their hostility toward one another with them to the New World.

Throughout the 1680s and 1690s battles took place between the French and the British settlers. Both sides tried to enlist the help of the Iroquois. The British were generally more successful in winning the Iroquois to their side. In 1692, for example, the Iroquois attacked the French village of Verchères, located along the St. Lawrence, 22 miles (35 km) below Montreal. If it had not been for the coolheaded bravery of fourteen-year-old Madeleine de Verchères, all of the inhabitants of the settlement might well have been killed. In the face of the panic all around her, young Madeleine took charge, rationed the food and water, and kept the settlement in order until reinforcements could get there.

By the time of the outbreak of the imperial wars between the French and the British, the patterns of settlement along the river had been established. Native Americans were being pushed out by European settlers. These settlers were farmers and fishermen, fur traders and merchants, lumberjacks and shipbuilders. Their origins were both French and English. Although the English would win out in the end, the river from the Gulf to Montreal would remain French-Canadian in character. The names of river settlements testify to the triple heritage of Native American, French, and British. English towns like Kingston and Cornwall share the river with French towns such as Trois-Rivières and Baie St. Paul. Although the native name, Hochelaga, has been replaced by the French name, Montreal, two native names remain as the names of the country and its capital, Canada and Ottawa. Many of the French names for towns, for example, Trois-Saumons (Three Salmon) and Rivière-du-Loup (River of the Wolf) were adopted from native stories about the region.

CHAPTER FOUR

POLITICAL DEVELOPMENT

When the battles between the English and the French began in the 1600s, no one could have predicted that the final result of these wars would be the creation of two new nations that would share the St. Lawrence River. But that is what happened. The warfare between the British and the French led finally to the development of Canada and the United States as independent nations.

The British and the French had been enemies for many, many years. They were both monarchies (that is, they had kings and queens as heads of their governments), and they both wanted many of the same things, especially new colonies and new markets in which to trade their products. England and France were close neighbors. Only the tiny strip of water known as the English Channel separated them. Frequently, the closer countries are located to each other, the more suspicious they are of each other. This was certainly true of France and England. What is more, they had developed very different religions. In the 1400s, 1500s, and 1600s, people often went to war over the question of religious beliefs. It is not so surprising, then, that the French and British citizens carried their hatred of each other to North America.

Even before Europeans began to settle in the New World, people from the Basque, a region in France, had fished in the waters around the mouth of the St. Lawrence. As early as 1500, French sailors found this water to be rich in whales, animals valued at that time for their oil, which was used in lighting lamps. Because of this fishing, the French were used to thinking of the Canadian wilderness as belonging to them. They did not care that French settlers had not established towns throughout the territory known as New France. After all, Cartier had claimed it for France. For the French, that was enough.

The British disagreed. Although many English people fished for a living, the British were mainly interested in settlement. Wherever there was wilderness, the British believed that the first people to establish a village or town were free to claim the land. As they began to move north from their cities and towns in New York and New England, they pushed into territory that was claimed by the French. This led to frontier battles that often coincided with major wars that were taking place between the two countries back home in Europe. In 1629, when Champlain was still alive, the British first managed to capture Quebec City. The French regained it by treaty in 1632. Because of the location of this city, high on a point overlooking one of the narrowest sections of the river, the control of this point meant the control of the entire St. Lawrence River valley. Throughout the late 1600s and early 1700s, the French carefully guarded Quebec and constructed several other forts up and down the river to defend against invaders.

Another very important strategic point in the battles for the North American continent lies in the Gulf of St. Lawrence. This is Louisbourg on Cape Breton Island. From the fort at Louisbourg the French could guard against a British fleet entering the St. Lawrence River by way of the Atlantic Ocean. From the 1720s until 1745, when the fort was captured by the British, Louisbourg was a key part in the defense of New France.

Until 1756 the fighting between the British and the French in North America was confined to frequent but inconclusive skirmishes. First one side would win, and then the other would win. Trouble always seemed to break out, but full-scale warfare had not really occurred on the North American continent. Then in 1756 England and France began a war called the Seven Years' War. In America, where much of the fighting took place, the conflict was called the French and Indian War.

In North America the name was different because there were very different participants in this part of the war. The Native Americans who had willingly helped the English in earlier battles had begun to mistrust their former English friends. So, when this new war broke out, many tribes agreed to help the French. They believed that the French with their emphasis on fur trading and fishing were not going to disrupt the native way of life nearly as much as were the English. The British fenced the land for farms and established towns and cities instead of simple trading posts.

The war raged on for many years. The most important victory, however, was the capture of Quebec City in 1759. A Canadian legend has grown up around this battle and the two young generals who fought it. James Wolfe led the British troops, and Montcalm led the French. Because of the loss of Louisbourg before the war had even begun, the French were vulnerable to an Atlantic attack. Then, early in the war, the French lost Fort Frontenac, which had protected them from British invasion by way of Lake Ontario. Before the French knew it, the British had sailed to the very gates of Quebec City. Montcalm and his troops were still safe, however, because it seemed as though no army could scale the rock cliffs to the city. They had not counted on the clever General Wolfe. By a series of careful maneuvers and lucky accidents, he found an access to the cliff-top city. British troops defeated the French on the field known as the Plains of

*General Wolfe led the British assault
on French-held Quebec City in 1759.*

Abraham just outside Quebec City. During the battle both Wolfe and Montcalm were killed.

The war lasted four more years, but when the French and British leaders sat down to work out a peace treaty, the battle of Quebec determined what they would write. As of 1763 and the Treaty of Paris, New France no longer existed. Now Canada and the St. Lawrence River were part of British North America. Almost all of the French possessions in the New World passed into the hands of the English.

This was not the end of war for the people along the St. Lawrence River. Less than fifteen years later, the American Revolution broke out. Some of the people living in North America wanted their freedom from the British king, George III. Most of the people living in Canada remained loyal to the king, and again the St. Lawrence River became a critical battlefront. The British stationed troops north of the river and used Canada as a base of operations from which to attack the rebels in the New England colonies. Colonists in northern New York, Vermont, New Hampshire, and Maine wanted to push the British back, far north of the river, so that the new nation they were forming would own all of the St. Lawrence River.

This was not to be. Although the British lost the fight to keep their thirteen Atlantic colonies, they held on to Canada and to most of the St. Lawrence River. Although the present boundary was not firmly established until the Webster-Ashburton Treaty in 1842, the St. Lawrence became a part of the border between British Canada and the new United States at the end of the American Revolution.

Loyalists—American colonists who did not want to fight against the king of England—fled to Canada after the war. Most of them established their homes along the banks of the St. Lawrence in what is now the Province of Ontario. A reconstructed village showing what life was like at that time has been built just outside Brockville, Ontario. Called Upper Canada Village because of its location along the upper portion of the St. Lawrence River, this historical site attracts many visitors each year.

In 1812 one more war focused the world's attention on Canada and the St. Lawrence River. In 1812 a group of angry, young American congressmen believed that England was violating the rights of United States merchant ships. To get even, they proposed that the United States should invade Canada and capture that country. They were especially interested in gaining possession of the St. Lawrence River. The so-called War of 1812 lasted almost three years, but neither side gained any territory from the other side when the war ended. The most important outcome of the war was the recognition by both England and the United States that the wealth of the St. Lawrence River could be tapped by both countries peacefully.

Since the signing of the Treaty of Ghent in 1815, there has been no warfare between Canada and the United States. Soon after the War of 1812, the British began to prepare Canada for independence. On July 1, 1867, Canada became a separate nation. Since 1867 the United States and Canada have shared the longest unarmed peaceful boundary in the world. The St. Lawrence River and the Great Lakes are vital parts of that border.

One group of people has not shared in the prosperity of the United States and Canada, even though the river and all the land once belonged to them. These are the Iroquois, Algonquins, Huron, and other Native Americans. Because they sided with the French during the later imperial wars, these people found themselves on the losing side when peace came. Neither the British nor the American colonists treated them kindly. Eventually, the Native Americans were pushed onto reservations. Today, most of their descendants live on these reservations located along the St. Lawrence. Although they have special hunting and fishing rights, their lives on the reservations are plagued by poverty, unemployment, and disease. They are proud people, who are trying to preserve their ancestral ways. Life on the reservations, however, is strictly controlled by the governments of Canada and the United States. In some places where the reservation crosses the international boundary, the tribes fall under the regulations of both nations.

Caughnawaga is a Mohawk reservation across from the Lachine Rapids on the southern bank of the river. Here on the site of Fort St. Louis, Roman Catholic priests have sung the church liturgy in the Mohawk language for several centuries. Upstream from Caughnawaga, where the southern shore becomes United States property, there is another Mohawk reservation, the Akwesasne, or "land where the partridge drums." This reservation spreads over fifty islands and touches both Canadian and American soil. At one time the world's finest lacrosse sticks were made on the Akwesasne reservation. Today the people of this reservation are most famous for their courage and skill in working on high-rise construction. Periodically they leave the reservation and travel to cities to help build towering skyscrapers. Most often, when the job is through, they return to their homes on the banks of the river.

CHAPTER
FIVE

THE
SEAWAY

Whenever people have seen the St. Lawrence River, they have invented ways to travel on it. Native American canoes, the *goélettes* of the Gaspé, the *bateaux* of the coureurs de bois, the wooden sailing ships of the early settlers, British and French warships, and hundreds of Canadian and American commercial vessels have plied the waters of the St. Lawrence. Until 1959 all of them had met many of the same obstacles. Above Montreal for a stretch of some 200 miles (320 km), the river churned with dangerous rapids. Farther on, in searching for a passage from the river to the Great Lakes, people had to solve the problem of bypassing Niagara Falls and the various other drops in sea level as they progressed from lake to lake.

As early as the eighteenth century, people tried to construct a continuous waterway from the Gulf of the St. Lawrence to the Great Lakes. In 1700, French priests built the first of many canals around the Lachine Rapids at Montreal. By building a canal, they could bypass the rapids. The process of entering and leaving the canal was time-consuming, and ships had to be small in order to fit, but it could be done.

The Welland Canal around Niagara Falls was the second step in enabling people to have continuous passage from the Atlantic Ocean to the Great Lakes. Chartered by the Province of Ontario in 1824, the Welland Canal ran from St. Catharines to Port Colbourne and allowed ships to go around Niagara Falls. When the Welland Canal opened, the first ships were able to pass from Lake Ontario to Lake Erie. The largest natural barrier on the waterway had been bypassed.

By the middle of the nineteenth century, the friendship between the United States and Canada meant that the St. Lawrence River had lost its military significance. At the same time, the economic importance of the river was growing dramatically. Lumber had replaced fur as the leading product of the Canadian north woods, and a way was sought to ship lumber products and other raw materials from Canada directly to Europe and the growing midwestern cities of the United States. If this could be accomplished, inland ports like Montreal, Quebec City, Buffalo, and Cleveland could become centers of international trade.

In 1854 the United States and Canada signed a treaty allowing the products of each nation to pass without tariffs up and down the St. Lawrence. One year later the first ship passed through the locks at Sault Ste. Marie. Nicknamed "the Soo," this series of locks was built to enable ships to pass from Lake Michigan to Lake Superior. Another step in the continuous waterway had been completed.

By 1908, ships with a draft no deeper than 14 feet (4.2 m) could travel from Montreal through the Great Lakes. In 1950 this situation had not changed even though a large portion of Canada's trade traveled along this route. The trip was very slow and involved passage through a great number of locks. Cargoes had to be unloaded from big ocean freighters at Montreal and packed onto smaller river freighters for the remainder of the

Opened in 1829, the Welland Ship Canal skirted Niagara Falls
and was a beginning step in providing continuous passage along
the St. Lawrence from the Great Lakes to the Altantic Ocean.

*Twin locks of the modern "Soo"—the area between
Sault Ste. Marie, Michigan, and Sault Ste. Marie, Ontario, on
the St. Mary's River connecting Lakes Superior and Huron.*

trip. Tedious as the voyage was, however, it was an efficient and inexpensive way to move heavy cargo. But people dreamed of finding a way to let the ocean ships make the whole voyage. As early as 1825 a Montreal citizen named John Young had written about a "Seaway" that would allow large ships from the Atlantic to travel the entire 2,300 miles (3,680 km) up the St. Lawrence and through the Great Lakes to the westernmost point on Lake Superior.

In spite of the locks and canals that had been built by 1950, the natural barriers to this passage were enormous. At Montreal the St. Lawrence River is 22 feet (6.6 m) above sea level. Duluth, Minnesota, the farthest port city on Lake Superior, is 602 feet (181 m) above sea level. In order for large oceangoing vessels to travel from Montreal to Duluth, two huge engineering feats had to take place.

First, a deep channel had to be cut out of the river wherever it was too shallow for large ships to pass. Second, a series of locks had to be constructed to lift the ships up each new step of the rising water level and to lower them on the return trip. Old locks and canals had to be modernized, and the harbors along the river and lakes would have to be deepened.

Canada had long been interested in this project. As a first step, her government had rebuilt the Welland Canal in 1932. Eight locks allowed ships 80 feet (24 m) wide, 859 feet (257.7 m) long, and 30 feet (9 m) deep to bypass Niagara Falls. This new canal was big enough for ocean freighters.

In July 1932, the United States Congress considered a joint agreement with Canada called the St. Lawrence Deep Waterways Treaty. Under this treaty a 27-foot (8.1-m) channel would be constructed all the way from Montreal to the Great Lakes. At the same time a mammoth hydroelectric-power project would be built using the waterpower from the rapids. Power generated by this project would fuel homes and businesses in New York and Ontario.

Not everyone in the United States thought this was a good

idea, and the Senate defeated the treaty in 1934. Atlantic seacoast companies were afraid they would lose business to this new Seaway. After all, if the Seaway was completed as planned, Buffalo, New York, would be closer to Liverpool, England, than New York City would be. Surely this would hurt New York's shipping business. Other Atlantic ports and harbors on the Gulf of Mexico agreed. In addition, railroads in the Midwest were worried about their businesses. So were private utility companies and coal companies that did not want to compete with the inexpensive hydroelectric power from the Seaway project.

In March 1941, the American supporters of the Seaway urged President Franklin Roosevelt to propose the Seaway again. He did. Plans for the Seaway might have begun at this time except that World War II interrupted everything. When the war ended, Canada decided to go ahead with its own plans for the development of a seaway. Finally, on May 13, 1954, according to the terms of the Wiley-Dondero Act, the United States Congress agreed to join Canada in building both the Seaway and the power project. At long last the dream of a continuous waterway from the Atlantic Ocean to the Great Lakes could be realized.

Although every city along the river and the lakes had separate jobs to do to get ready for the ocean freighters, the bulk of the construction took place in a 200-mile (320-km) section of the river between Montreal and the Thousand Islands. This stretch includes the 114 miles (182 km) of the St. Lawrence River that mark the border between the United States and Canada. This is why it was so important that the two nations work together.

The locks at Sault Ste. Marie and Niagara Falls were sufficient to handle ocean ships. The task ahead was to construct a third set of locks on the St. Lawrence River between Montreal and the Thousand Islands. By the time the job was completed, the whole project had taken four years and cost about one billion dollars. Over twenty thousand people worked on the Seaway, and they used seventy million dollars' worth of equipment to do their jobs.

*The Eisenhower Lock near Massena, New York,
shown here with construction well underway,
was one of seven new locks built in the 200-mile
stretch between Montreal and the Thousand Islands.*

First the river had to be drained in sections where the channel would be deepened. This was a hazardous job because of the fast rapids and the harsh winters. As each section was drained, a temporary cofferdam was built to hold other parts of the river back away from the drained area. Once the water was drained out, huge ditchdiggers had to carve out a deep channel so that when the water was allowed to flow back into that part of the river, the channel would be deep enough for ocean liners to pass through.

One of the most amazing machines used in this work was a mechanical excavator known as the "Gentleman." The "Gentleman" weighed 650 tons (589 tonnes). For a machine with such a polite name, it did not have a very dainty appetite. The "Gentleman" ate over 25 tons (22.7 tonnes) of rock and clay in every bite, and it took a bite every forty-eight seconds. All together it ate 2,000,000 tons (1,814,000 tonnes) in six months.

Machines with the strength of the "Gentleman" were necessary because of two geological formations found on the river's bottom. One was a kind of clay that the engineers working on the Seaway nicknamed the "blue goop." Another was the glacial rock that had been left behind by the Ice Age. This rock was so hard that it stripped the teeth from power shovels after they had been digging only twelve hours.

Besides the hard glacial rock and the "blue goop," the people working on the Seaway faced another natural obstacle—the cold winter. The project could not stop during the winter months, but the work at that time was hard going. Metal tools froze and snapped off. Earth and gravel froze solidly to truckbeds and had to be warmed before the loads could be dumped. Workers' hands froze to tools and frostbite was a constant worry. An ice jam near the Long Sault in 1957 almost ripped out the dam in that area. Because of these hazards, engineers learned to use glacial till instead of concrete as a building material. A mixture of pebbles, sand, and clay, the glacial till stayed free of cracks in sub-zero cold.

In addition to digging the channel, new locks had to be built. The Côte Ste.-Catherine and St.-Lambert locks were built opposite Montreal to bypass the Lachine Rapids. Just above Montreal the Upper and Lower Beauharnois Locks were built. These two locks lift incoming ships 84 feet (25.2 m) to the level of Lake St.-Francis. Next, two more locks had to be built in the river near Massena, New York. These two locks, the Snell and Eisenhower locks, lift ships again, this time onto the 28-mile (45-km)-long Lake St. Lawrence. This lake was created as part of the Seaway when engineers flooded the Long Sault Rapids, once the wildest rapids on the river. Passing out of Lake St. Lawrence, ships needed to be routed through one final river lock, the Iroquois Lock. The completed Seaway had seven new river locks, five in Canadian waters and two on the American side. Ships using these locks could be 730 feet (219 m) long and 75 feet (22.5 m) wide and could weigh 29,000 tons (26,303 tonnes). When the Seaway opened in 1959, eighty percent of the world's ships met these specifications.

The creation of the Seaway meant new business opportunities for people in cities along the St. Lawrence and Great Lakes. However, it also meant a great disruption in the lives of many of the people living in small towns and villages. Seven small villages had to be flooded completely by the Seaway. Aultsville, Farran Point, Dickinsons Landing, Wales, Milles Roches, Moulinette, and Iroquois, all villages in Canada, were buried under the river forever. Over 6,500 people had to move from their houses to make way for the Seaway project.

Queen Elizabeth II and President Dwight D. Eisenhower attended the official opening ceremonies of the Seaway on June 26, 1959.

On July 1, 1958—Dominion Day, Canada's day of independence—the cofferdams holding back the water from Lake St. Lawrence were blasted away. Three days later on the American Independence Day, the Fourth of July, the first ocean freighter steamed down the new channel. The Seaway would not officially open until the following year, but the mighty project was completed. At the official opening ceremonies in 1959, the prime minister of Canada and the president of the United States were joined by the queen of England. These three heads of state represented three of the four great nations whose history had been changed by the St. Lawrence River. The insignia of the St. Lawrence River Development Corporation combines an eagle, a maple leaf, and Neptune's trident. The trident stands for the river, the maple leaf stands for Canada, and the eagle stands for the United States. Two nations working together on the banks of the river they share had managed one of the greatest engineering feats of all time.

CHAPTER
SIX

ECONOMIC
DEVELOPMENT

The ways of making a living along the shores of the St. Lawrence River are as varied as the people who have inhabited these shores. Fur trading and fishing were the first great industries. Fur trading ended when the beaver died out along the river, but fishing is still a thriving multimillion-dollar business.

Because fishing is central to their way of life, the people who live along the Gaspé Peninsula have long been called "the true children of the St. Lawrence." Their main catch is cod. Passing through villages like Cloridorme on the Gaspé, you can see clothesline after clothesline of codfish drying in backyard breezes. Although the codfishers no longer prepare their catch in outdoor ovens, much of their lives remains the same as it was in their great-great-grandparents' time. The villages on the Gaspé were settled by Bretons, French people who were used to a life by the open sea.

Inland, on rivers that feed into the St. Lawrence, today's descendants of these Bretons catch salmon. Île d'Anticosti, located in the middle of the river, is said to have the best salmon

*Logs en route to Trois-Rivières, Canada,
nicknamed the "Newsprint Capital of the World."*

fishing in the world. On the banks of the smaller rivers, Gaspé farmers raise sheep that are highly prized in the famous restaurants of Montreal and Quebec City. On menus Gaspé sheep is called *aigneau pré-salé* (French for presalted lamb) because of the delicate taste the salty sea air gives to the sheep as they graze on the riverbank. Other Gaspé industries include woodcarving and shipbuilding. At St.-Joseph-de-la-Rive, *goélettes* were once constructed. These were special 75-foot (22.5-m)-long hand-crafted Gaspé fishing boats.

Across from the Gaspé is the north coast of the St. Lawrence River, an area so rocky and barren that Cartier called this the "land of Cain." In 1948, however, rich iron lodes were discovered in Labrador, and the few lone fishing villages that had clung to the north coast for centuries boomed into mining towns. They became port cities for the export of iron ore as well as for the aluminum and titanium that have been discovered in this metal-rich area. Tadoussac, once a trading post for Basque whalers, is now the site of one of the world's largest aluminum plants. Situated at the mouth of the Saguenay where that river flows into the St. Lawrence, Tadoussac is also the home of a hydroelectric plant that produces more power than either the Hoover or the Grand Coulee dams. Sept-Îles, once a sleepy fishing village, has developed into Canada's third-largest port since the discovery of iron ore in Labrador.

The Canadian north woods yield another product that has long gone to market by way of the St. Lawrence. This is lumber. Whole towns exist along the river because of the lumber industry and its sister industry, paper production. The cathedral at Baie-Comeau looms over a harbor choked with pulp boats loaded with barked pine, spruce, and balsam. Until the opening of the Seaway these boats were no larger than Cartier's flagship, *Hermine*. Entire families work in the pulp business and sometimes live on the pulp boats. Eleven miles (17.6 km) away, Trois-Rivières is the leading lumber city in Canada and the "Newsprint Capital of the World." Over a hundred million logs annually enter Trois-Rivières, many traveling the short distance from Baie-Comeau by a water flume. Once a tiny fort in Champlain's wilderness defense system, Trois-Rivières now has plants that produce over a thousand tons of newsprint daily. Fittingly, the Provincial School of Papermaking is located here.

Trois-Rivières is located midway between Montreal and Quebec City, the two largest Canadian cities on the St. Lawrence. Both of these cities are French, as is most of the Province of Quebec. Until recently, English was the official language of the province, even though fewer than fifteen percent of Quebec's inhabitants spoke English as their native tongue. The cities of Montreal and Quebec are leaders in the struggle to have French Canada truly recognized by the national government. Some extreme patriots of the province would like Quebec to be separate from the rest of Canada. If they were to succeed, very little of the St. Lawrence River, the "Mother of Canada," would remain in Canadian hands.

For now, Quebec City is the capital of the Province of Quebec. While Canada was owned by the British, Quebec City was the area's leading timber port. In 1825 the world's then largest ship, *Baron Renfrew*, called at her port. Quebec is the oldest major city in Canada. One of her hospitals has remained in operation since 1637. Her first monastery was established in 1663 and first convent, in 1717. Today Quebec City is one of Canada's leading industrial centers. Industries here produce textiles, pulp, and paper, chemical, and mineral products.

In the midnineteenth century, advances in steam power and the dredging of Montreal harbor meant that this city surpassed Quebec as a river port. It has kept the lead ever since. Originally settled by a group of mystics led by Sieur de Maisonneuve, Montreal developed more slowly than Quebec City. However, as the coureurs de bois brought furs down the Ottawa River to Montreal, the city ceased to be a religious retreat and began its life as a bustling commercial center. By water Montreal is closer to England than New York City is. Montreal today is the second largest port in Canada and handles well over $300 million a year in shipping. A cosmopolitan, modern city, Montreal claims petroleum refining, clothing, pharmaceuticals, and meat-packing as her leading industries.

Montreal and Quebec City may be the leading cities on the river proper, but since the opening of the Seaway, many other cities in both Canada and the United States have had their prosperity closely tied to river commerce. In Canada both Hamilton and Toronto in the Province of Ontario look to the lakes and the river for much of their business. At Hamilton huge steel and chemical plants stand right on the banks of Lake Ontario, ready to have their products shipped east to the Atlantic or west to the American agricultural heartland. Toronto, slightly less accessible than Hamilton, shares the shore of Lake Ontario. Toronto's major industries are printing and publishing, meat-packing, chemicals, and the production of electrical machinery, metal products, and furniture.

The Seaway opened up inland Great Lakes ports for the United States as well as for Canada. Five of the most important of these were Buffalo, New York; Cleveland, Ohio; Chicago, Illinois; Milwaukee, Wisconsin; and Detroit, Michigan. When the Seaway opened in 1959, sixty percent of the population of Canada and the United States lived within 500 miles (800 km) of Buffalo. Buffalo was the largest milling center in the world and the nation's largest steel center. The Seaway meant that grain from the Midwest could be sent by ship to Buffalo, processed, and then sent on for sale in Europe. The Seaway also meant that iron ore from the new fields in Labrador could be shipped to the Buffalo factories. Other general cargo from specialized Buffalo industries— player-piano rolls, merry-go-round horses, Wurlitzer organs— could be sent to Europe far more cheaply by the new water route.

What the Seaway could do for Buffalo, it could do doubly for Chicago. Long the nation's largest trucking and rail center, Chicago now had a third method of transportation by which to send the agricultural and industrial products of the midwestern United States. Tractors could be sent to Norway by the Seaway for three-fourths the cost of transportation in pre-Seaway days. Road-building machines could be sent to England for twenty percent less than before. Likewise, Chicago was able to import European goods at substantial savings.

Milwaukee had been prepared for the Seaway as early as 1908. In that year the city changed its Lake Michigan sandbar into a waterfront. Milwaukee hoped to become one of the country's major inland ports. Although Milwaukee does not ship as many tons as other Seaway ports, the cargo from this city is among the most varied and valuable shipped along the waterway. Today Milwaukee's major industries are meat-packing, beer, and the production of automotive parts and diesel and gasoline engines.

Cleveland and Detroit are two other industrial cities in the chain along the Seaway. Cleveland had been known for its steel and chemical plants long before the Seaway opened. As was the case for Buffalo, the Seaway meant for Cleveland easy water access to the iron from Labrador. The Seaway also meant easier shipment of Cleveland's products, such as electric motors, paint, rubber, and plastic. Detroit has always been the "Car Capital" of the United States. With the opening of the Seaway, Detroit was able to ship new cars to Europe, to Canada, and to ports in the United States by means of huge oceangoing freighters. Detroit also serves as an export center for packaged food products headed to Europe.

Both before and after the construction of the Seaway, tourism was a major industry all along the St. Lawrence River. People interested in sportfishing visit even the tiny villages along the north bank of the Gulf of St. Lawrence. As early as 1864 a hotel in Les Escoumins sheltered four Confederate soldiers. La Malbaie, known to the English as Murray Bay, was once called the "Newport of the North." Here many famous people, including one United States president, have had summer homes.

*A ship laden with iron ore passes through the
McArthur Locks on the "Soo." Over sixty million tons
of iron ore are shipped annually through the
Soo Locks, much of it bound for the steel ports
of Buffalo and Cleveland.*

*Boldt Castle on Heart Island is a popular
Thousand Islands tourist attraction with a
romantic past. Built by a wealthy hotel owner
for his wife, the German-style castle
was to be a "summer cottage." When the wife
died in 1902, work stopped and the castle
stands unfinished to this day.*

Of all the tourist attractions on either side of the river, how-ever, none can compare with the Thousand Islands. Frozen over and desolate in winter, these green islands come alive in the blue water of the St. Lawrence when the ice goes out. Some of the summer camps on these islands are no more than shacks. Others are elaborate homes complete with servants' quarters. Boldt's Castle in the Thousand Islands stands unfinished, the epitome of a fancy nineteenth-century "summer cottage." Legends abound in these islands about characters such as Admiral Bill Johnston, a pirate of the nineteenth century, and his daughter, Kate, "Queen of the Thousand Islands." Legends abound, too, about the great muskellunge, huge fish that are caught each summer in this part of the river. Everyone who catches a 40-pound (18.14-kg) "muskie" dreams of catching one that weighs 50 pounds (22.68 kg).

Whether the tourists come searching for muskie, an island paradise, or a place to water-ski is unimportant. What is impor-tant is that they return to the St. Lawrence summer after sum-mer, making tourism a profitable livelihood for the area's year-round inhabitants.

CHAPTER SEVEN

ECOLOGY AND THE SEAWAY

The development of the Seaway, the industrial growth of the region, and the expansion of tourism have all changed the St. Lawrence River. Most of these changes have been good ones, but there have been some changes that are not so good.

When Cartier first sailed up the mouth of the St. Lawrence, he was astounded by the numbers of wonderfully strange animals he saw. The river was full of whales and porpoises, more than he had ever seen in any other waters. Here Cartier saw walruses for the first time. Writing about these animals in his diary, he described them as "fish in appearance like horses which go on land at night."

The walruses are gone now from the St. Lawrence, and so are most of the whales. The people who live along the shores of the river have been responsible for their disappearance. At Île aux Coudres whales were once caught by the dozens by means of mazes constructed in the river. In the 1930s the Quebec government put a bounty on belugas, small white whales that were attracted by the rich marine life at Tadoussac, near the mouth of the Saguenay. People fishing in the area had complained that the whales were depleting their catch. By means of the bounty law, Quebec paid them to kill the belugas, and these whales were almost exterminated.

The earliest example of man's extermination of animals along the St. Lawrence occurred during the time of the French fur trade. Beavers do not reproduce themselves very rapidly. Naturalists have estimated that if beavers were left all alone to die naturally, their population would only increase by about twenty percent. There were perhaps ten million beavers in North America when the Europeans arrived. The beavers' habits made them easy prey for the traders. Beavers always return to their homes. All the trappers had to do was wait. By 1635 the beavers had all but vanished as far up the river as Trois-Rivières. The fur trade finally ended when the trappers could no longer easily find their furry victims.

Even in the Thousand Islands where good fishing is still a major tourist attraction, old-timers argue that there are not nearly as many muskellunge and other big fish as there once were. Walleyed pike once swam by the thousands in this part of the river. Since the 1950s they have been so scarce as to seem almost nonexistent. Residents of the area blame the Seaway and the ocean freighters for pollutants that have killed off the schools of walleyes and other fish.

People who are upset about the death of these fish are very concerned about a new Seaway proposal. Seaway officials have been examining plans that would allow them to keep the entire waterway open all winter long. To destroy the ice in the river permanently would mean the destruction of several small islands. A group called "Save the River" has formed to protest this plan. They argue that keeping the river flowing all winter would disturb the natural cycle for wildlife. They claim that the breakup of the small islands would destroy wildlife homes. Wave activity would erode the shoreline and wash out nests and feeding areas. The opponents of the winter Seaway also argue that ships pass enough pollutants into the water during the months the Seaway is now open. Why add more, they wonder.

When the initial plans for the Seaway were developed, not too many people thought about the ecological effects of changing the river's pattern. That thinking has changed. There are formal areas where wildlife is preserved, such as the Wilson Hill Game Management Area, where hundreds of Canadian geese find refuge each year.

As people have become more ecologically aware, many individual attempts have been made to protect the environment for birds, fish, and other animals. Although the St. Lawrence may no longer be home to the numbers and varieties of wildlife that surprised Cartier on his early voyages, there are still many animals to be seen along its banks and in its water. Quebec farms still carry "weir rights," the legal permission to fish from the banks of riverfront farms. And Quebec farmers still catch lots of fish, including prized speckled trout. In the Gulf of St. Lawrence an international effort is being made to rescue the harp seals before this species becomes extinct. Whale watchers can still set out from Tadoussac and come home satisfied at having seen these water mammals at play. Loons and kingfishers swoop over the mills at Trois-Rivières. Each year over two hundred thousand snow geese land at Cap Tourmente.

In the Thousand Islands, fishing and hunting yield rich rewards even if you don't catch a giant muskie. All kinds of bass, northern pike, and perch swim there, together with scaup, buffleheads, goldeneyes. The blue heron soars overhead, sharing the sky with such common birds as the red-winged blackbird, the woodcock, pintail ducks, and killdeer. Other Thousand Island birds include the eastern kingbird, the ring-billed gull, the tufted titmouse, the spotted sandpiper, and the godwit.

For the animals and people living along the St. Lawrence and

Increased economic development of the Seaway poses many threats to the natural environment. The rerouting of the river and pollution from heavy shipping have already harmed natural habitats, and unless future plans take into account ecological concerns, certain fish and other wildlife may face extinction.

the Great Lakes, water pollution is a constant problem. Concern about water pollution has greatly changed the way people look at shipwrecks, accidents that at one time were the material for romantic legends. Historians estimate that at least ten thousand wrecks lie at the bottom of the St. Lawrence. When the river was dredged during the construction of the Seaway, bulldozers unearthed countless cannon balls, hulls, and anchors, mute testimony to ships that had gone down on the river.

Some wrecks are more famous than others. Most Canadian schoolchildren know of HMS *Lowestoffe*, the first British vessel to sail upriver with the news of Wolfe's victory at Quebec. The *Lowestoffe* hit some rocks and sank off the north bank of the river. An earlier wreck was that of a Basque galleon that sank, loaded with whale oil, close to the mouth of the river. Some of the sailors may have survived, because when Cartier landed in the New World, he found Native Americans who spoke a few Basque words.

Basque whalers sinking in the river returned whale oil to its watery home. Today when an oil tanker runs aground and spills its cargo into the river, people worry. Unlike whale oil, petroleum spreads out on top of the water, destroying beaches, killing fish, and preventing waterbirds from flying. When an oil spill occurs, it takes many people and many dollars to repair the damage. And each time, some birds and fish die. One such spill on the St. Lawrence River in 1976 was the largest oil spill in United States history to that date.

Both the United States and Canada are concerned about ecology along the route of the Seaway. They have decided to work together for the preservation of the environment. In 1971 both nations signed a Water Quality Agreement, by which they pledged to abide by mutual standards for clean water. There is some evidence that their efforts to reduce the levels of poisonous mercury in fish in the St. Lawrence and Great Lakes have already begun to pay off.

In the 1980s new pollutants—especially chemical waste products—challenge the international environmentalists. Acid rain is another problem. Along with smaller bodies of water in Ontario, Quebec, and the Adirondacks, the St. Lawrence is slowly being poisoned by rain that contains dangerous chemicals. All these problems can be overcome, and working together is the only way to solve them. Seaway officials have promised that they will undertake no new projects without first consulting ecologists about the effects such projects might have on the river and its wildlife.

CHAPTER EIGHT

THE FUTURE OF THE WATERWAY

When the St. Lawrence Seaway was completed in 1959, people called it grandiose names. Some said it was North America's "Fourth Seacoast." Others said it was the "North American Mediterranean." Still others claimed its title should be "The Eighth Sea." Unfortunately the Seaway has not yet lived up to the promise of these names. For example, the waterway has not yet begun to pay back to Canada and the United States the millions that it cost to build. In 1980 twenty-five percent of United States foreign trade touched the area around the Seaway, but less than ten percent of that trade traveled by way of the Seaway's ships.

Why is the Seaway having these problems? First, although it is still less expensive to ship heavy materials by water, the cost of this form of transportation has risen substantially in recent years because of the mounting tolls charged by the Seaway. Rates have more than doubled since the Seaway opened. Second, the most profitable materials to send by sea are those that shippers call bulk cargo—wheat, coal, and iron ore. These products have always accounted for over three-fourths of the Seaway's business. During the early 1970s the Seaway experienced a slight boom when Soviet freighters began carrying North American grain home to their country. Except for this spurt, however, the last two decades have not been growth years for the Seaway's major products. The steel industry in the northeastern United States, particularly in lake ports like Buffalo and Cleveland, has fallen on hard times, and its iron needs have been greatly reduced. Coal use has been outstripped in many areas by the use of other kinds of fuel. When the Seaway opened, its supporters predicted that it would do 50,000,000 tons (45,350,000 tonnes) of business by 1960. Throughout the 1970s the Seaway had to struggle to meet that mark, even with the longer shipping year effected by new air-bubble icebreakers.

When the Seaway's engineers planned the size of the locks and channels, they felt that they were accommodating the largest ships necessary. However, ships have changed since 1959. Today, much of the world's crude oil travels on huge supertankers. These and high-speed containerized freighters cross the Atlantic Ocean very quickly. Even if they could fit in the locks along the Seaway, it is more profitable for them to avoid that time-consuming journey and simply unload their cargoes at Atlantic seaports, from where the cargoes are transported inland by truck or rail.

To these technical problems have been added two other problems that all northeastern industry, not just the Seaway, has faced in recent years. One is the changing pattern of trade and the new emphasis on high-technology industry like computers, rather than on older, traditional heavy industries. With this change has come a shift in population within the United States, from the northeastern cities to southern and western cities of the so-called Sun Belt. Buffalo is no longer the geographic center for American business that it was in the 1950s.

A second related problem has been the high cost of labor and the frequency of strikes. During one stretch in the early 1970s, ships sat idle for many weeks, waiting for the dockers' strike to end so that their cargoes could be unloaded.

The Seaway may never be the commercial success that people predicted it would be. Nevertheless, it still stands as a monument to cooperation between human beings and nature and between the people of two different nations. The Seaway was a mighty project for a mighty river.

The St. Lawrence River has seen many business ventures come and go, from the first fur trade to the ocean traffic of today. Through it all, the river flows on, steadily carrying its load of water from the Great Lakes to the Atlantic Ocean.

Although the Seaway has not yet fulfilled the expectations of its planners, it has made the St. Lawrence a vital economic link, forged by the cooperation of the two nations that share its banks.

INDEX

Above (navigation term), 6, 8
Algonquin Indians, 14, 17, 26
American Revolution, 25

Below (navigation term), 6, 8
Borders, 13, 25, 26
British settlement, 18–26
Buffalo, N.Y., 43, 55

Canada, 13, 15, 17, 21, 26
Canals, 28–29, 32
Cartier, Jacques, 4, 14–15, 17
Champlain, Samuel de, 15, 17
Chicago, Ill., 43–44
Cities, 42–44
Cleveland, Ohio, 44

Detroit, Mich., 44
Drainage area, 6

Ecology, 48–53

Economic development, 18, 29,
  39–47
Erie, Lake, 4, 5, 29
Estuary, 9
European settlement, 14–26

Fishing, 9, 39, 41, 48–49, 50
Flatland, 9, 11
Formation of river, 8
Forts, 4, 22, 23
French and Indian War, 23–25
French settlement, 14–25
Fur trade, 18, 39, 49
Future of Seaway, 54–57

Gaspé Peninsula, 9, 39, 41
Great Lakes, 4, 5, 6, 17, 28–38,
  43
Gulf of St. Lawrence, 8, 22

Huron, Lake, 5

Ice Age, 8
Icebreakers, 9
Indians, 3, 14, 17–18, 20, 23, 26–27
Industry, 39–47, 54, 55
International Rapids, 11
Iroquois Indians, 3, 14, 17, 20, 26

Landmarks, 4, 25
Louisbourg, 22–23
Lumber, 41–42

Michigan, Lake, 5, 29
Milwaukee, Wis., 44
Mohawk Indians, 3, 18, 27
Montcalm, 4, 23, 25
Montreal, 4, 11, 15, 20, 42, 43
Mouth, 5–6, 8

Navigation, 11, 28, 29, 32
    terms, 6, 8
Niagara Falls, 29, 30

Ontario, 25, 43
Ontario, Lake, 4, 5, 6, 29, 43

Political development, 21–27
Pollution, 52–53

Quebec, 17, 22, 23, 25, 42

Quebec City, 8, 42

Rapids, 11
Religion, 17–18, 21–22
River pilots, 1–4

St. Lawrence Seaway, 3, 28–38,
    48–57
Salt water, 8, 9
Settlement, European, 14–26
Source, 5, 8
Superior, Lake, 5, 29

Thousand Islands, 11, 13, 47,
    49, 50
Toronto, 43
Tourism, 44, 47
Treaties, 25, 26, 29, 32
Tributaries, 6
Trois-Rivières, 4, 8, 42

United States, 13, 21, 26

Voyageurs, 17

War of 1812, 26
Weather, 9
Wildlife, 48–50
Wolfe, James, 3, 23, 25

ABOUT
THE
AUTHOR

Trudy Hanmer grew up on the banks of the St. Lawrence, in Massena, New York. All her early summers were spent in a camp on the river that was flooded when the Seaway was built.

She is a graduate of Wellesley College and holds a Masters degree in history from the University of Virginia. Ms. Hanmer is Associate Principal of the Emma Willard School in Troy, New York. She still enjoys fishing and boating on the St. Lawrence.